# UNITED STATES NAVY PATCHES

SUBMARINES

MICHAEL L. ROBERTS

**Schiffer Military/Aviation History**
Atglen, PA

## Acknowledgements

I would like to recognize a few friends that are authorities on U.S. Navy submarines:

| | |
|---|---|
| Barry Commons | Dave Robinson |
| Jim Millholland | James Townley |


The patches depicted in this book are from the author's personal collection and are presented to serve as a guide for historians and collectors.

This book is not intended to be the complete authority on the subject. It depicts over 650 patches from World War II to the present.

The images on pages 6, the front cover and endsheets are official U.S. Navy photographs.

---

Book Design by Michael L. Roberts & Robert Biondi.


Library of Congress Catalog Number: 96-69997



Printed in Hong Kong.
ISBN: 0-7643-0186-1



Published by Schiffer Publishing Ltd.
77 Lower Valley Road
Atglen, PA 19310
Phone: (610) 593-1777
FAX: (610) 593-2002
Please write for a free catalog.
This book may be purchased from the publisher.
Please include $2.95 postage.
Try your bookstore first.

# Foreword

Insignias are the modern form of heraldry of the knights of old. In the armed services insignias serve as a form of shorthand that identifies an individual's service, rank, authority, specialty and organization. The organizational insignia, from the plain to very involved design, expresses a pride in oneself and his or her organization. From this pride springs self-discipline, the essence of respect for self, for service and for country.

The first semi-official Navy organizational insignias began to appear in the fledging Naval Aeronautical Organization in the early twenties with the establishment of the Bureau of Aeronautics in 1921 and a year later the formation of fighting, scouting, observation, seaplane patrol and torpedo plane squadrons. By 1927, the now familiar High Hat, Felix the Cat and VF-2's Flying Chiefs squadron insignias began appearing on the sides of the Navy's nimble, brightly colored biplane fighters. By the beginning of World War II all Navy aviation squadrons, most Naval and Reserve air stations, and even aircraft carriers had distinctive insignias.

During the Second World War aviation squadrons, surface ships and submarines, and shore establishment organizational insignias abound, establishing a high esprit de corps within each individual in that unit. Donald Duck, Mickey Mouse, Bugs Bunny and a host of other characters truly went to war with all branches of the armed services on the sides of tanks, planes and ships bridges. In fact in 1943, the Navy told its squadrons to knock off using Donald Duck so often for proposed insignias.

I remember all the displays of insignias in *Life* Magazine ads and collecting bottle caps and stickers from boxes of cereal during the war that had aviation insignias on them. We all knew what the insignias of the Flying Tigers, Eagle squadron, 94th Fighter and VF-31 squadrons looked like, what kind of planes they flew and how they performed in combat. When I grew up I was able turn my childhood dream into reality when I became a Naval Aviator. Acquiring that first patch in Training Squadron One and having it sewn on my flight jacket meant I had arrived and was truly a part of that unit. As my career progressed, so did the number of patches on my flight jacket until I ran out of room. Each patch on my jacket, as well as those that adorn the jackets of my fellow Naval Aviators, aircrew, and squadron/ship mates have a special memory and, in many cases, a long history behind them.

My interest in insignias is historical and I was fortunate to be able to continue to gather information on Navy and Marine Corps aviation organizations while I was in the Navy. Frequent trips to Washington, D.C., allowed me to spend considerable time at the Naval Air and Operational Histories offices where I collected as much information as I could on Navy/Marine squadrons. I have been lucky to be able to be in a position to share much of this information as insignia editor for THE HOOK magazine, the Tailhook Association's quarterly journal of carrier aviation. In this capacity I have produced the magazine's patch page, a feature for 16 years, and answered all insignia inquiries. I quickly learned that it is next to impossible to identify every insignia because there are so many, and many are unidentifiable, even with the help of the historians at the Naval Air History office where all Navy aviation insignias are supposed to be officially approved.

This book serves as a valuable guide for the insignia collector and lovers of Navy patches in providing color pictures of past and present active and Reserve Navy aviation squadrons, ships, aircraft and shore organizations. It will help the serious collectors and those getting started to identify patches in their collections. Mike's collection of Navy insignias is vast and I thank him for sharing his collection with all of us.

Doug Siegfried, CDR USN (Ret)
THE HOOK Magazine
Insignia Editor

# Contents

# UNITED STATES NAVY PATCHES

CSDG-1, Unmanned Vehicle Detachment

CSDG-1, Unmanned Vehicle Detachment

NR-1

NR-1, Challenger Salvage/Recovery, 1986

NR-1

NR-1

## RESEARCH & RESCUE

Mystic (DSRV-1)

Avalon (DSRV-2)

Mystic (DSRV-1)

Avalon (DSRV-2)

Trieste (DSV-1)

Turtle (DSV-3)

Turtle (DSV-3)

Sea Cliff (DSV-4)

USS USS Mackerel (SST-1)

USS Barracuda (SST-3)

USS Narwhal (SS-167)

USS Nautilus (SS-168)

USS Porpoise (SS-172) USS Tarpon (SS-175)

USS Pickerel (SS-177) USS Permit (SS-178)

USS Pollack (SS-180)

USS Skipjack (SS-184)

USS Snapper (SS-185)

USS Stingray (SS-186)

USS Sturgeon (SS-187)

USS Sturgeon (SS-187)

USS Sargo (SS-188)

USS Spearfish (SS-190), Battle Flag

USS Sailfish (SS-192)

USS Seawolf (SS-197)

USS Tambor (SS-198)

USS Gudgeon (SS-211)

USS Gato (SS-212)

USS Greenling (SS-213)

USS Grouper (SS-214)

USS Barb (SS-220)

USS Blackfish (SS-221) USS Bluefish (SS-222)

USS Cod (SS-224) USS Cod (SS-224)

## SUBMARINES

USS Cero (SS-225)

USS Darter (SS-227)

USS Drum (SS-228)

USS Flying Fish (SS-229)

USS Flying Fish (SS-229), Battle Flag

USS Finback (SS-230)

USS Haddock (SS-231)

USS Shad (SS-235)

USS Silversides (SS-236)    USS Silversides (SS-236)

USS Whale (SS-239)    USS Angler (SS-240)

USS Angler (SS-240) — USS Bashaw (AGSS-241)

USS Bluegill (SS-242) — USS Bluegill (SSK-242)

USS Brean (SS-243) USS Cavalla (SS-244)

USS Cobia (SS-245) USS Croaker (SS-246)

USS Croaker (SS-246), 8000 Dives

USS Flasher (SS-249)

USS Gabilan (SS-252)

USS Muskallunge (SS-262)

## SUBMARINES

USS Pogy (SS-266)

USS Pogy (SS-266)

USS Rasher (SS-269)

USS Rasher (AGSS-269)

USS Raton (SS-270)

USS Ray (SSR-271)

USS Redfin (SS-272)

USS Sawfish (SS-276)

USS Sawfish (SS-276) USS Scorpion (SS-278)

USS Tunny (APSS-282) USS Tunny (SS-282)

USS Tunny (SSG-282) USS Balao (SS-285)

USS Billfish (SS-286) USS Bowfin (SS-287)

USS Cabrilla (SS-288)

USS Cabrilla (SS-288)

USS Cabrilla (SS-288), Battle Flag

USS Crevalle (SS-291)

USS Crevalle (SS-291)

USS Devilfish (SS-292)

USS Dragonet (SS-293)

USS Ling (SS-297)

USS Ling (SS-297) USS Lionfish (SS-298)

USS Sabalo (SS-302) USS Sablefish (SS-303)

USS Aspro (SS-309) USS Batfish (SS-310)

USS Batfish (SS-310) USS Archerfish (AGSS-311), Operation Seascan

USS Archerfish (AGSS-311), USS Burrfish (SSR-312)

USS Burrfish (SS-312) USS Perch (SS-313)

USS Perch (APSS-313)

USS Perch (APSS-313)

USS Sealion (SS-315)

USS Barbero (SS-317)

**SUBMARINES**

USS Barbero (SSG-317)

USS Barbero (SSG-317)

USS Baya (AGSS-318)

USS Becuna (SS-319)

## SUBMARINES

USS Becuna (SS-319)

USS Bergall (SS-320)

USS Blackfin (SS-322)

USS Blackfin (SS-322)

USS Criman (SS-323) USS Blenny (SS-324)

USS Blower (SS-325) USS Boarfish (SS-327)

USS Bugara (SS-331)

USS Bullhead (SS-332)

USS Bumper (SS-333)

USS Cabezon (SS-334)

USS Carbonero (SS-337)

USS Carbonero (SS-337)

USS Carbonero (SS-337), Westpac, 1965

USS Carp (SS-338)

USS Carp (SS-338)

USS Catfish (SS-339)

USS Catfish (SS-339)

USS Catfish (SS-339)

USS Catfish (SS-339)

USS Entemedor (SS-340)

USS Entemedor (SS-340)

USS Chopper (SS-342)

USS Clamagore (SS-343) USS Cobbler (SS-344)

USS Cochino (SS-345) USS Corporal (SS-346)

USS Cubera (SS-347)

USS Cusk (SS-348)

USS Cusk (SS-348)

USS Diodon (SS-349)

USS Dogfish (SS-350)

USS Dogfish (SS-350)

USS Dogfish (SS-350)

USS Greenfish (SS-351)

USS Greenfish (SS-351) USS Halfbeak (SS-352)

USS Halfbeak (SS-352) USS Golet (SS-361)

USS Guavina (SS-362)

USS Guitaro (SS-363)

USS Hardhead (SS-365)

USS Hardhead (SS-365)

USS Icefish (SS-367) USS Jallao (SS-368)

USS Kete (SS-369) USS Kraken (SS-370)

USS Lamprey (SS-372) | USS Lamprey (SS-372)

USS Lizardfish (SS-373) | USS Menhaden (SS-377)

**SUBMARINES**

USS Sand Lance (SS-381)

USS Picuda (SS-382)

USS Picuda (SS-382)

USS Pampanito (SS-383)

USS Parche (SS-384)

USS Bang (SS-385)

USS Bang (SS-385)

USS Pilotfish (SS-386)

USS Piranha (SS-389) USS Pomfret (SS-391)

USS Sterlet (SS-392) USS Sterlet (SS-392)

## SUBMARINES

USS Sterlet (SS-392) USS Razorback (SS-394)

USS Razorback (SS-394) USS Redfish (SS-395)

USS Redfish (SS-395)

USS Ronquil (SS-396)

USS Ronquil (SS-396)

USS Scabbardfish (SS-397)

USS Segundo (SS-398)

USS Sea Cat (SS-399)

USS Sea Cat (SS-399), Battle Flag

USS Sea Devil (SS-400)

USS Seadog (SS-401) USS Seadog (SS-401), Straits of Formosa, 1945

USS Seafox (SS-402) USS Seafox (SS-402)

**SUBMARINES**

USS Atule (SS-403) USS Spikefish (SS-404)

USS Sea Owl (SS-405) USS Sea Owl (SS-405)

USS Sea Poacher (SS-406)

USS Sea Robin (SS-407)

USS Sea Robin (SS-407)

USS Sennet (SS-408)

USS Piper (SS-409)

USS Threadfin (SS-410)

USS Threadfin (SS-410)

USS Trepang (SS-412)

USS Spot (SS-413)

USS Springer (SS-414)

USS Stickleback (SS-415)

USS Tiru (SS-416)

USS Tench (SS-417) USS Tench (SS-417)

USS Thornback (SS-418) USS Tigrone (SS-419)

USS Tirante (SS-420)

SS Trutta (SS-421)

USS Toro (SS-422)

USS Torsk (SS-423)

USS Torsk (SS-423), 50th Anniversary, 1944-1994

USS Quillback (SS-424)

USS Quillback (SS-424)

USS Trumpetfish (SS-425)

USS Trumpetfish (SS-425) USS Tusk (SS-426)

USS Corsair (SS-435) USS Corsair (SS-435)

USS Argonaut (SS-475)

USS Argonaut (SS-475)

USS Runner (SS-476)

USS Conger (SS-477)

USS Conger (SS-477)

USS Cutlass (SS-478)

USS Cutlass (SS-478)

USS Cutlass (SS-478)

USS Diablo (SS-479)

USS Diablo (AGSS-479)

USS Requin (SS-481)

USS Requin (SSR-481)

USS Irex (SS-482) USS Sea Leopard (SS-483)

USS Odax (SS-484) USS Sirago (SS-485)

USS Pomodon (SS-486)

USS Remora (SS-487)

USS Remora (SS-487)

USS Sarda (SS-488)

USS Sarda (SS-488) USS Spinax (SSR-489)

USS Volador (SS-490) USS Gudgeon (SS-507)

USS Amber Jack (SS-522) USS Grampus (SS-523)

USS Pickerel (SS-524) USS Grenadier (SS-525)

USS Dolphin (SS-555) USS Dolphin (SS-555)

USS Dolphin (AGSS-555) USS Tang (SS-563)

USS Trigger (SS-564)

USS Wahoo (SS-565)

USS Wahoo (SS-565)

USS Trout (SS-566)

USS Gudgeon (SS-567) USS Harder (SS-568)

USS Albacore (SS-569) USS Nautilus (SSN-571)

USS Sailfish (SS-572)

USS Sailfish (SSR-572)

USS Salmon (SS-573)

USS Salmon (SSR-573)

USS Grayback (LPSS-574)

USS Grayback (SSG-574)

USS Seawolf (SSN-575)

USS Darter (SS-576)

## SUBMARINES

USS Darter (SS-576)

USS Darter (SS-576), 1956-1989

USS Growler (SSG-577)

USS Skate (SSN-578)

USS Skate (SSN-578), Westpac, 1985

USS Swordfish (SSN-579)

USS Barbel (SS-580)

USS Barbel (SS-580)

USS Blueback (SS-581) — USS Blueback (SS-581), Westpac, 1982

USS Bonefish (SS-582) — USS Bonefish (SSR-582)

USS Bonefish (SS-582), UNITAS XX, 1979

USS Sargo (SSN-583)

USS Sargo (SSN-583)

USS Seadragon (SSN-584)

USS Skipjack (SSN-585) USS Skipjack (SSN-585)

USS Skipjack (SSN-585) USS Triton (SSN-586)

USS Triton (SSRN-586) USS Halibut (SSN-587)

USS Halibut (SSGN-587) USS Scamp (SSN-588)

USS Scamp (SSN-588), UNITAS XIX, 1978

USS Scorpion (SSN-589)

USS Scorpion (SSN-589)

USS Sculpin (SSN-590)

USS Shark (SSN-591)

USS Snook (SSN-592)

USS Snook (SSN-592), Mediterranean Run, 1981

USS Snook (SSN-592), UNITAS XXI, 1980

USS Thresher (SSN-593)

USS Permit (SSN-594)

USS Permit (SSN-594), Westpac Patrol, 1975-1976

USS Plunger (SSN-595)

USS Barb (SSN-596) USS Barb (SSN-596)

USS Tullibee (SSN-597) USS George Washington (SSBN-598)

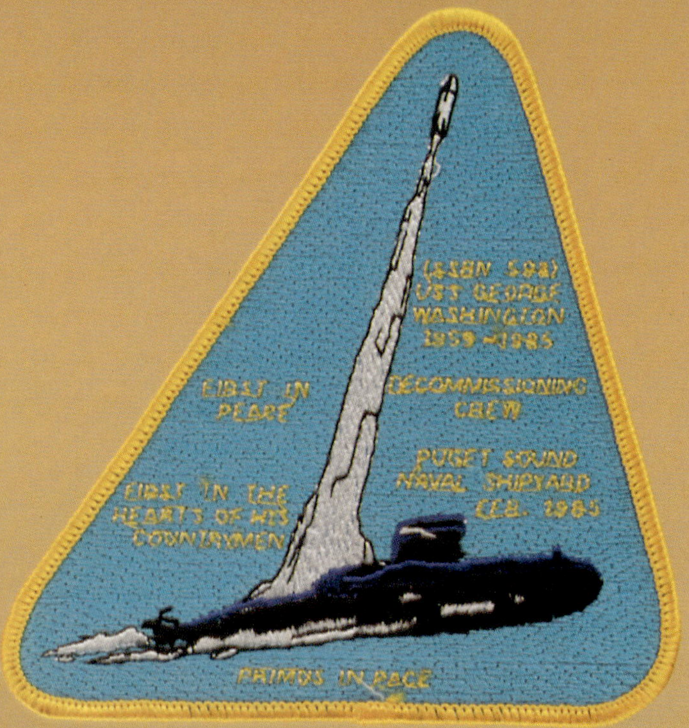


USS George Washington (SSN-598), UNITAS XXIV, 1983

USS George Washington (SSBN-598), Decommisioning Crew, 1985

USS Patrick Henry (SSBN-599)

USS Theodore Roosevelt (SSBN-600)

USS Robert E. Lee (SSBN-601)

USS Abraham Lincoln (SSBN-602)

USS Pollack (SSN-603)

USS Pollack (SSN-603)

USS Pollack (SSN-603), Northern Pacific, 1987

USS Pollack (SSN-603), Northern Pacific, 1987

USS Haddo (SSN-604)

USS Haddo (SSN-604)

USS Haddo (SSN-604), Westpac, 1979

USS Haddo (SSN-604), Westpac, 1985

USS Jack (SSN-605)

USS Jack (SSN-605), Mediterranean Cruise, 1979-1980

USS Jack (SSN-605), Mediterranean Run, 1981

USS Tinosa (SSN-606)

USS Tinosa (SSN-606), UNITAS XXIII, 1982

USS Dace (SSN-607)

USS Ethan Allen (SSBN-608) USS Sam Houston (SSBN-609)

USS Thomas A. Edison (SSBN-610) USS John Marshall (SSBN-611)

USS John Marshall (SSN-611) USS Guard Fish (SSN-612)

USS Flasher (SSN-613) USS Flasher (SSN-613)

USS Greenling (SSN-614) USS Greenling (SSN-614), Mediterranean Cruise, 1981-1982

USS Greenling (SSN-614), Mediterranean Run, 1983-1984 USS Greenling (SSN-614)

USS Gato (SSN-615)

USS Lafayette (SSBN-616)

USS Lafayette (SSBN-616), 25 Years, 1963-1988

USS Alexander Hamilton (SSBN-617)

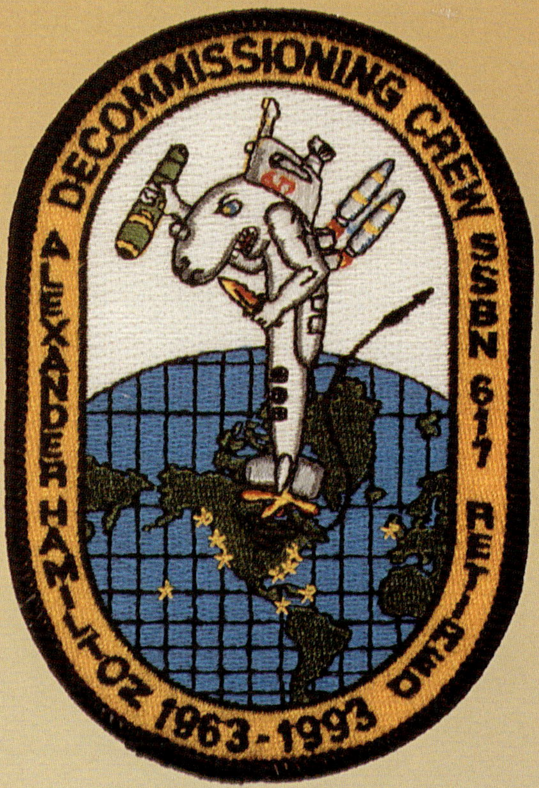


USS Alexander Hamilton (SSBN-617)

USS Alexander Hamilton (SSBN-617)

USS Alexander Hamilton (SSBN-617), Decommisioning Crew, 1963-1993

USS Alexander Hamilton (SSBN-617), Decommisioning Crew, 1963-1993

USS Thomas Jefferson (SSBN-618)

USS Thomas Jefferson (SSBN-618)

USS Thomas Jefferson (SSN-618), Decommisioning Crew, 1963-1985

USS Andrew Jackson (SSBN-619)

USS John Adams (SSBN-620)

USS Haddock (SSN-621)

USS Haddock (SSN-621), Westpac, 1981

USS James Monroe (SSBN-622)

USS Nathan Hale (SSBN-623) USS Nathan Hale (SSBN-623), 20th Anniversary, 1963-1983

USS Woodrow Wilson (SSBN-624) USS Henry Clay (SSBN-625)

USS Henry Clay (SSBN-625), Final Patrol, 1977, Gold Crew

USS Daniel Webster (SSBN-626)

USS James Madison (SSBN-627)

USS Tecumseh (SSBN-628)

USS Tecumseh (SSBN-628) USS Tecumseh (SSBN-628)

USS Daniel Boone (SSBN-629) USS Daniel Boone (SSBN-629), C-4 Backfit, 1984

USS John C. Calhoun (SSBN-630)

USS John C. Calhoun (SSBN-630), Atlantic Fleet Outstanding FBM Award, 1988

USS John C. Calhoun (SSBN-630), 1000th Patrol

USS Ulysses S. Grant (SSBN-631)

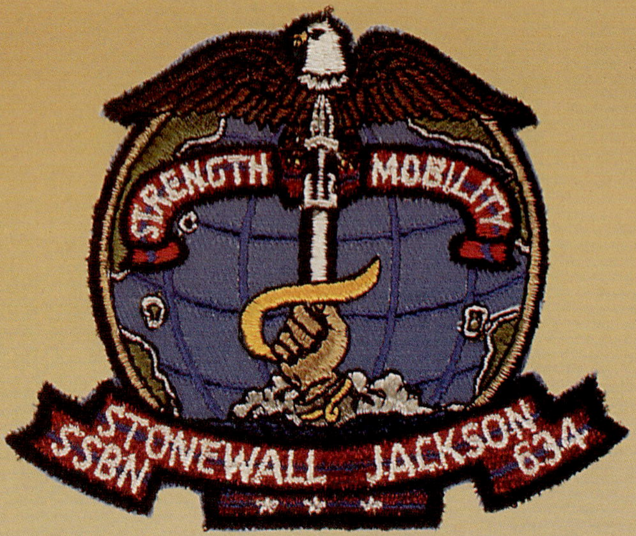


USS Von Steuben (SSBN-632)

USS Casimir Pulaski (SSBN-633)

USS Casimir Pulaski (SSBN-633)

USS Stonewall Jackson (SSBN-634)

USS Sam Rayburn (SSBN-635)

USS Nathanael Greene (SSBN-636)

USS Nathanael Greene (SSBN-636)

USS Nathanael Greene (SSBN-636), Blue Crew

USS Sturgeon (SSN-637) USS Whale (SSN-638)

USS Whale (SSN-638) USS Tautog (SSN-639)

**SUBMARINES**

USS Tautog (SSN-639)  USS Tautog (SSN-639), Westpac, 1980

USS Benjamin Franklin (SSBN-640)  USS Benjamin Franklin (SSBN-640), 50th Patrol, Gold Crew, 1983

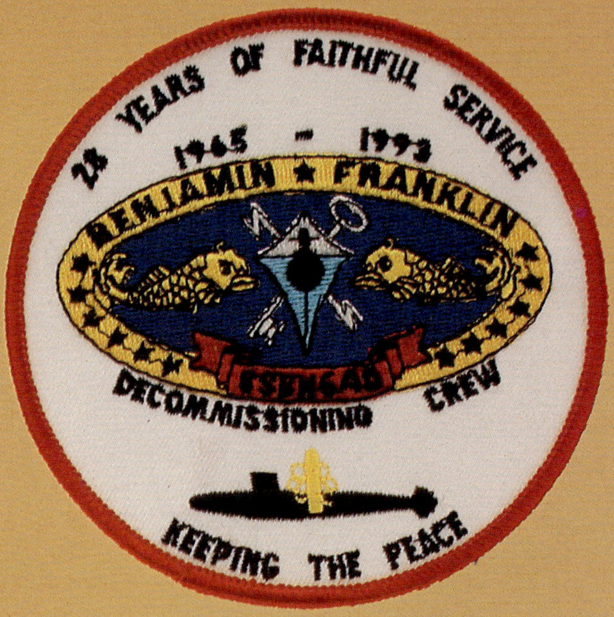


USS Benjamin Franklin (SSBN-640), Patrol 69

USS Benjamin Franklin (SSBN-640), Decommisioning Crew, 1965-1993

USS Simon Bolivar (SSBN-641)

USS Simon Bolivar (SSBN-641), 25th Anniversary, 1965-1990

USS Kamehameha (SSBN-642)

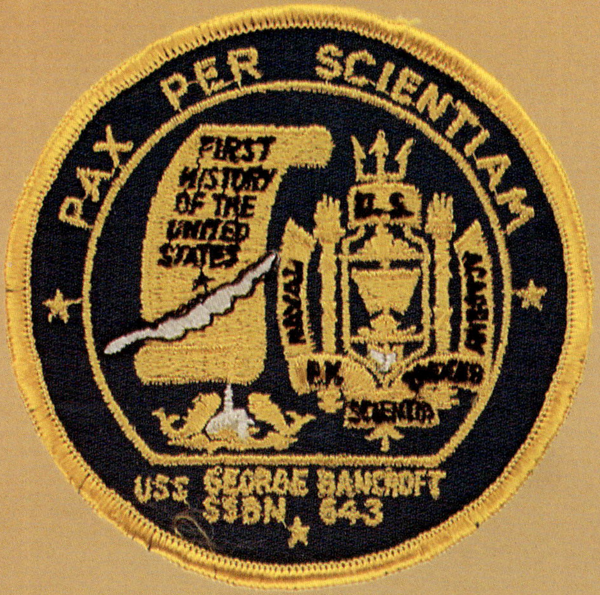


USS George Bancroft (SSBN-643)

USS George Bancroft (SSBN-643)

USS George Bancroft (SSBN-643)

USS George Bancroft (SSBN-643), 50th Patrol

USS Lewis & Clark (SSBN-644)

USS Lewis & Clark (SSBN-644)

USS James K. Polk (SSBN-645)

USS James K. Polk (SSBN-645), Four for Freedom, Gold Crew

USS James K. Polk (SSN-645)

USS Grayling (SSN-646)

USS Grayling (SSN-646)

USS Grayling (SSN-646), Northern Run

USS Grayling (SSN-646), Mediterranean Run, 1981

USS Grayling (SSN-646), Mediterranean, 1983

USS Grayling (SSN-646)

USS Pogy (SSN-647)

USS Pogy (SSN-647), Overhaul, 1980-1981

USS Pogy (SSN-647), Holiday Run, 1991-1992

USS Pogy (SSN-647), Westpac, 1995

USS Aspro (SSN-648)

USS Aspro (SSN-648)

USS Sunfish (SSN-649)

USS Pargo (SSN-650)

USS Queenfish (SSN-651) USS Queenfish (SSN-651), Westpac, 1972-1973

USS Puffer (SSN-652) USS Ray (SSN-653)

USS George C. Marshall (SSBN-654)

USS Henry L. Stimson (SSBN-655)

USS Henry L. Stimson (SSBN-655), Overhaul, 1982-1984

USS George Washington Carver (SSBN-656)

USS Francis Scott Key (SSBN-657) — USS Mariano G. Vallejo (SSBN-658)

USS Mariano G. Vallejo (SSBN-658) — USS Mariano G. Vallejo (SSBN-658), 4 for 4

USS Mariano G. Vallejo (SSBN-658), 8 for 8, Blue Crew, 1978

USS Will Rogers (SSBN-659)

USS Sand Lance (SSN-660)

USS Lapon (SSN-661)

USS Gurnard (SSN-662)

USS Hammerhead (SSN-663)

USS Hammerhead (SSN-663), 1776-1976

USS Hammerhead (SSN-663), Northern Run, 1979

USS Hammerhead (SSN-663), Top of the World Tour, 1990 USS Sea Devil (SSN-664)

USS Sea Devil (SSN-664) USS Guitarro (SSN-665)

USS Hawkbill (SSN-666)

USS Hawkbill (SSN-666), Equator/Westpac, 1985

USS Bergall (SSN-667)

USS Bergall (SSN-667)

## SUBMARINES

USS Bergall (SSN-667), Holy Loch/Faslane/Hallifax, 1980-1981 USS Spadefish (SSN-668)

USS Spadefish (SSN-668), Mediterranean, 1990 USS Spadefish (SSN-668), Icex, 1992

USS Spadefish (SSN-668), Icex, 1993 | USS Seahorse (SSN-669)

USS Finback (SSN-670) | USS Finback (SSN-670)

USS Finback (SSN-670), AUTEC, 1983 SS Finback (SSN-670), Mediterranean Cruise, 1982-1983

USS Narwhal (SSN-671), Blue USS Pintado (SSN-672)

USS Pintado (SSN-672), Icex, 1981

USS Flying Fish (SSN-673)

USS Flying Fish (SSN-673), Mediterranean Run, 1989-1990

USS Trepang (SSN-674)

USS Trepang (SSN-674)

USS Bluefish (SSN-675)

USS Bluefish (SSN-675), Mediterranean, 1979

USS Billfish (SSN-676)

USS Drum (SSN-677)

USS Drum (SSN-677), Westpac, 1974-1975

USS Drum (SSN-677), Westpac, 1984

USS Archerfish (SSN-678)

USS Archerfish (SSN-678), Icex, 1986

USS Archerfish (SSN-678)

USS Silversides (SSN-679)

USS Silversides (SSN-679), Icex, 1981

USS Silversides (SSN-679), Speed Run, AUTEC, 1984

USS Silversides (SSN-679), Decommissioning Crew, 1972-1994

USS William H. Bates (SSN-680)

USS Batfish (SSN-681)

USS Tunny (SSN-682)

USS Tunny (SSN-682)

USS Tunny (SSN-682), Westpac, 1986

USS Parche (SSN-683)

USS Cavalla (SSN-684)

USS Glenard P. Lipscomb (SSN-685)

USS Mendel Rivers (SSN-686)

USS Mendel Rivers (SSN-686), Icex, 1983-1984

USS Richard B. Russell (SSN-687)

USS Richard B. Russell (SSN-687), Christmas Cruise, Blue Crew, 1990

USS Richard B. Russell (SSN-687), Midpac, 1989

USS Richard B. Russell (SSN-687)

USS Richard B. Russell (SSN-687), Mission, 1991

USS Richard B. Russell (SSN-687), Mission, 1993

USS Los Angeles (SSN-688)

USS Los Angeles (SSN-688)

USS Los Angeles (SSN-688), Indian Ocean/Westpac, 1981

USS Los Angeles (SSN-688)

USS Los Angeles (SSN-688), Westpac, 1991

USS Baton Rouge (SSN-689)

USS Baton Rouge (SSN-689), Indian Ocean, 1980 — USS Philadelphia (SSN-690)

USS Philadelphia (SSN-690) — USS Memphis (SSN-691)

USS Memphis (SSN-691), AUTEC, 1983

USS Memphis (SSN-691), Pancake Patrol, 1984

USS Omaha (SSN-692)

USS Omaha (SSN-692)

USS Omaha (SSN-692), Westpac, 1984

USS Omaha (SSN-692), Norpac, 1991

USS Cincinnati (SSN-693)

USS Cincinnati (SSN-693), World Cruise, 1981

USS Cincinnati (SSN-693), Meditrranean Cruise, 1983-1984

USS Cincinnati (SSN-693), Mediterranean Run, 1988

USS Groton (SSN-694)

USS Groton (SSN-694)

## SUBMARINES

USS Groton (SSN-694), Around the World, 1980

USS Groton (SSN-694), World Cruise, 1980

USS Groton (SSN-694), Mediterranean Run, 1992

USS Birmingham (SSN-695)

USS Birmingham (SSN-695), AUTEC, 1983

USS Birmingham (SSN-695)

USS Birmingham (SSN-695), "E" and "A"

USS New York City (SSN-696)

## SUBMARINES

USS New York City (SSN-696), Norpac, 1988

USS New York City (SSN-696), Disaster Pac, 1991

USS Indianapolis (SSN-697)

USS Bremerton (SSN-698)

USS Jacksonville (SSN-699)

USS Jacksonville (SSN-699), Around the World, 1982

USS Dallas (SSN-700)

USS Dallas (SSN-700)

USS La Jolla (SSN-701)

USS Phoenix (SSN-702), Launch Crew

USS Phoenix (SSN-702)

USS Phoenix (SSN-702), World Cruise, 1983

USS Phoenix (SSN-702), AUTEC, 1984

USS Boston (SSN-703), Launch, 1980

USS Boston (SSN-703)

USS Baltimore (SSN-704), Launch, 1980

USS Baltimore (SSN-704)

USS Baltimore (SSN-704)

USS Corpus Christi (SSN-705), Launch, 1981

USS Corpus Christi (SSN-705)

USS City of Corpus Christi (SSN-705) USS City of Corpus Christi (SSN-705), AUTEC, 1983

USS Albuquerque (SSN-706) USS Portsmouth (SSN-707)

USS Minneapolis-St. Paul (SSN-708)

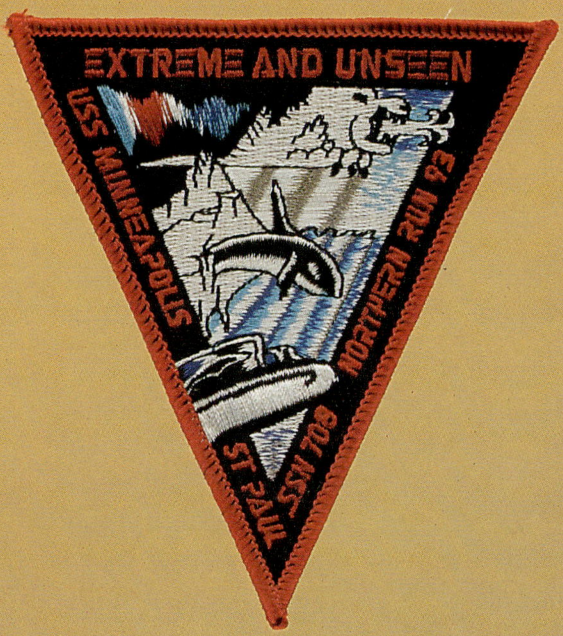


USS Minneapolis-St. Paul (SSN-708), Northern Run, 1993

USS Hyman G. Rickover (SSN-709)

USS Augusta (SSN-710)

USS San Fransisco (SSN-711), Launch, 1979

USS San Fransisco (SSN-711)

USS Atlanta (SSN-712), Launch, 1980

USS Atlanta (SSN-712)

USS Atlanta (SSN-712), AUTEC, 1982 — USS Atlanta (SSN-712), Mediterranean Cruise, 1987-1988

USS Atlanta (SSN-712), SINKEX, 1983 — USS Atlanta (SSN-712), Deployment, 1983

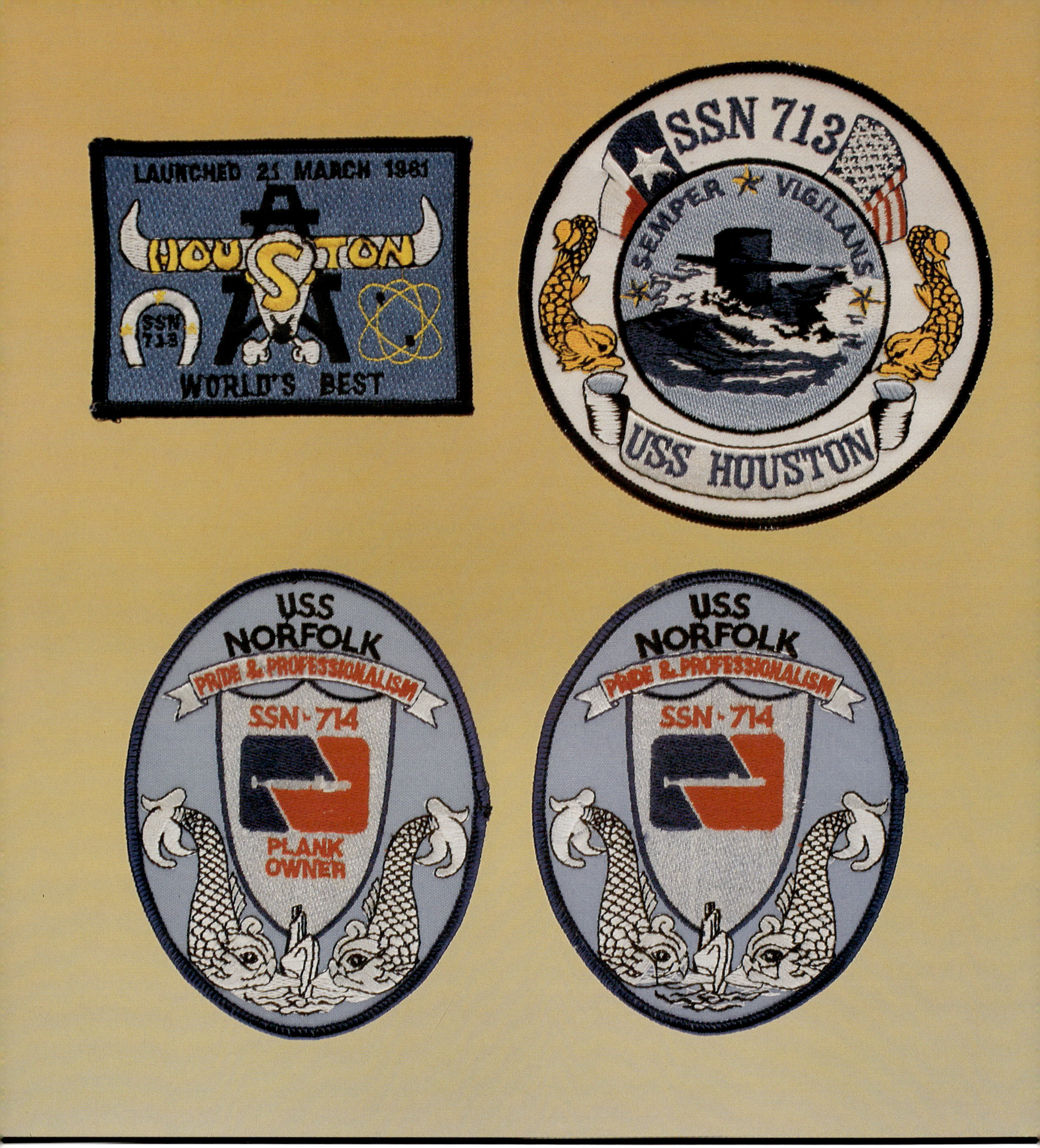


USS Houston (SSN-713), Launch, 1981

USS Houston (SSN-713)

USS Norfolk (SSN-714), Plankowner

USS Norfolk (SSN-714)

USS Norfolk (SSN-714) USS Buffalo (SSN-715), Launch, 1982

USS Buffalo (SSN-715) USS Salt Lake City (SSN-716)

USS Salt Lake City (SSN-716), Launch

USS Olympia (SSN-717)

USS Honolulu (SSN-718)

USS Providence (SSN-719)

USS Pittsburgh (SSN-720)

USS Chicago (SSN-721), cap patch

USS Chicago (SSN-721)

USS Key West (SSN-722)

USS Oklahoma City (SSN-723) | USS Oklahoma City (SSN-723)

USS Louisville (SSN-724), Launch, 1985 | USS Louisville (SSN-724)

USS Helena (SSN-725), Launch, 1986

USS Helena (SSN-725)

USS Helena (SSN-725)

USS Ohio (SSBN-726)

USS Ohio (SSBN-726)

USS Ohio (SSBN-726), First Patrol, Blue Crew, 1982

USS Michigan (SSBN-727)

USS Michigan (SSBN-727), Equatorial Crossing, Blue Crew, 1983

USS Michigan (SSBN-727), First Patrol, Gold Crew

USS Florida (SSBN-728), launch Crew

USS Florida (SSBN-728)

USS Florida (SSBN-728)

USS Florida (SSBN-728), Panama Canal, 1984

USS Georgia (SSBN-729)

USS Georgia (SSBN-729)

USS Henry M. Jackson (SSBN-730)

USS Alabama (SSBN-731), Launch Crew

USS Alabama (SSBN-731)

USS Alaska (SSBN-732), Launch Crew

USS Alaska (SSBN-732)

USS Alaska (SSBN-732) USS Nevada (SSBN-733), Launch

USS Nevada (SSBN-733) USS Tennessee (SSBN-734), Launch

USS Tennessee (SSBN-734)

USS Pennsylvania (SSBN-735), Patrol 13

USS Pennsylvania (SSBN-735)

USS Pennsylvania (SSBN-735), Patrol 15, cap patch

USS West Virginia (SSBN-736) USS Kentucky (SSBN-737)

USS Maryland (SSBN-738) USS Nebraska (SSBN-739)

USS Rhode Island (SSBN-740)    USS Maine (SSBN-741)

USS Wyoming (SSBN-742)    USS Newport News (SSN-750)

USS Newport News (SSN-750) | USS Newport News (SSN-750), Operation Desert Storm

USS San Juan (SSN-751) | USS Pasadena (SSN-752),Commissioning, 1989

USS Pasadena (SSN-752)

USS Pasadena (SSN-752)

USS Albany (SSN-753)

USS Topeka (SSN-754), PCU

USS Topeka (SSN-754)

USS Topeka (SSN-754), BSY-1

USS Miami (SSN-755)

USS Miami (SSN-755)

**SUBMARINES**

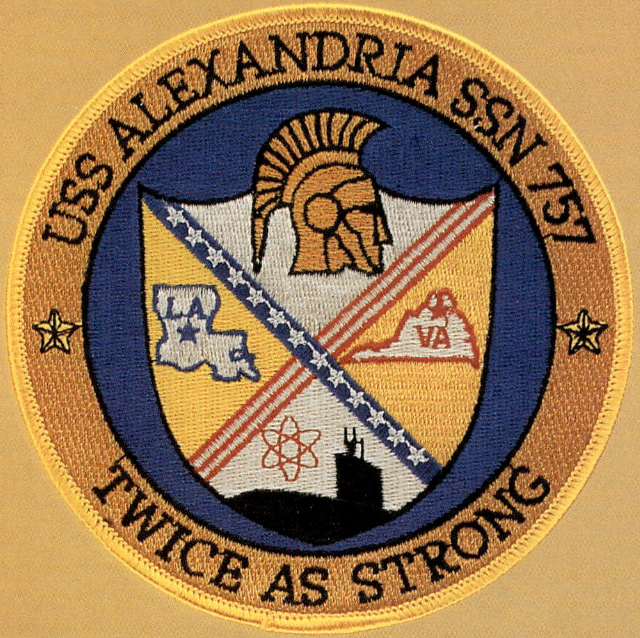

USS Scranton (SSN-756)

USS Alexandria (SSN-757)

USS Asheville (SSN-758)

USS Asheville (SSN-758), Westpac, 1994

USS Jefferson City (SSN-759)

USS Annapolis (SSN-760), Launch, 1991

USS Annapolis (SSN-760)

USS Springfield (SSN-761)

USS Columbus (SSN-762) USS Santa Fe (SSN-763)

USS Boise (SSN-764) USS Boise (SSN-764), Medpac, 1994-1995

USS Montpelier (SSN-765)

USS Charlotte (SSN-766)

USS Hampton (SSN-767)

USS Hartford (SSN-768), Launched, 1993

USS Hartford (SSN-768) USS Toledo (SSN-769)

USS Tucson (SSN-770) USS Columbia (SSN-771)

USS Greenville (SSN-772) USS Cheyenne (SSN-773)

USS Seawolf (SSN-21) USS Seawolf (SSN-21)

PSSN-TUFF

SMMS

Mermaid on Anchor

USS Fakefish, SSS-1

USS Neptune, SSN-525 (submarine for the movie *Grey Lady Down*)

# Index

PSSN-TUFF

SMMS

Mermaid on Anchor

USS Fakefish, SSS-1

USS Neptune, SSN-525 (submarine for the movie *Grey Lady Down*)

# INDEX

# GLOSSARY

| | |
|---|---|
| AGSS | Auxiliary Submarine (Diesel) |
| APSS | Transport Submarine (Diesel) |
| AUTEC | Acoustic Underwater Test and Evaluation Center |
| DSV | Deep Submergence Vehicle |
| DSRV | Deep Submergence Rescue Vehicle |
| Encapsulated Harpoon | Anti-Ship Missile (Submarine Launched) |
| IceEx | North Pole |
| LPSS | Amphibious Submarine (Diesel) |
| MedRun | Mediterranean Sea |
| MK-48 | Torpedo |
| NorPac | Northern Pacific |
| NR | Nuclear Research Submarine |
| PCU | Pre-Commissioning Unit |
| Polaris | Ballistic Missile (Submarine Launched) |
| Poseidon | Ballistic Missile (Submarine Launched) |
| SDV | Seal Delivery Vehicle |
| SinkEx | Ship Sinking Exercize |
| SS | Submarine (Diesel) |
| SSBN | Fleet Ballistic Missile Submarine (Nuclear) |
| SSG | Guided Missile Submarine (Diesel) |
| SSK | Anti-Submarine Submarine (Diesel) |
| SSN | Submarine (Nuclear) |
| SSR | Radar Picket Submarine (Diesel) |
| SSRN | Radar Picket Submarine (Nuclear) |
| SST | Training Submarine (Diesel) |
| SubLant | Submarine Atlantic |
| SubPac | Submarine Pacific |
| SubRoc | Anti-Submarine Rocket (Submarine Launched) |
| Trident | Ballistic Missile (Submarine Launched) |
| UNITAS | Annual exercise with South America |
| WestPac | Western Pacific |

*Also from the Publisher*

# UNITED STATES NAVY PATCHES

Volume I:
**Aircraft Carriers/Carrier Air Wings/Support Establishments**
Michael L. Roberts
Size: 8 1/2" x 11" over 1000 patches in color, index
160 pages, hard cover
ISBN: 0-88740-753-6 $29.95

Volume II:
**Aircraft/Attack Squadrons/Helicopter Squadrons**
Michael L. Roberts
Size: 8 1/2" x 11" over 1000 patches in color, index
144 pages, hard cover
ISBN: 0-88740-801-X $29.95

Volume III:
**Fighter/Fighter Attack/Reconnaissance Sqdns**
Michael L. Roberts
Size: 8 1/2" x 11" over 1000 patches in color, index
168 pages, hard cover
ISBN: 0-88740-802-8 $29.95

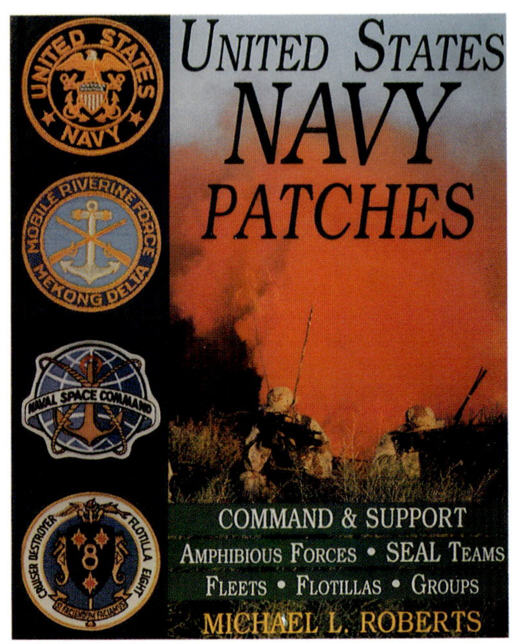


Volume IV:
**Command/Amphibious/SEAL Teams/Fleets/Misc. Formations**
Michael L. Roberts
Size: 8 1/2" x 11" over 1000 patches in color, index
160 pages, hard cover
ISBN: 0-7643-0068-7 $29.95